HEATHEN

Not one is not held in the arms of the rest, to blossom.
Not one is not given to ecstasy's lions.
Not one does not grieve.
Each of them opens and closes, closes and opens
the heavy gate—violent, serene, consenting, suffering it all.

—Jane Hirshfield from "The Lives of the Heart"

Heathen

Poems by
R. Flowers Rivera

LOTUS PRESS
Detroit

First Edition

International Standard Book Number 978-0-9797509-9-1

Printed in the United States of America

Lotus Press, Inc.
"Flower of a New Nile"
Post Office Box 21607
Detroit, Michigan 48221
www.lotuspress.org

for Klyne

ACKNOWLEDGMENTS

Grateful acknowledgment is made to the following publications in whose pages these poems first appeared, often in a slightly different form:

"Lady Tiresias: Seven Years a Woman," "Persephone: All Bound Up," "Isle of Promethea," and "Invoking Erato" in *UCity Review*; "Breckinridge Mill Dam" in *African American Review;* "Braiding Alexis" and "Ode to Sue" in *Feminist Studies;* "Salt" in *Barely South Review;* "I Am Hephaestus" in *Paper Darts*; "Doubt" and "Her" in *Wildflower Magazine*; "Jellyfish Heart" and "Trying to Explain" in *The Lindenwood Review;* "Aubade" (as "Predawn Aubade") and "Heavy in My Jesus Year" in *Forces;* "Charon the Ferryman," "Paris," "Ismene Speaks," and "E True Hollywood Story: M—" in *North Dakota Quarterly;* "Heathen" in *Janus Head* 6:2; "NY to Atlanta in Fourteen Hours" in *Glass Tesseract;* "Her Lover Eyes the Exit" and "The Red Eye of Dawn" in *Artisan: A Journal of Craft*; "Hera Has Her Say" and "A Siren Repents" in *The Southern Review;* "Salah: Dulles Airport" in *Janus Head;* "The Obtuse of a Literary Triangle" in *American Poets & Poetry;* "Invoking Erato" in *Lummox;* "Vivid" in *Janus Head;* "Ravished Landscapes" in *Cold Mountain Review*; and "Show, Don't Tell" in *Obsidian II: Black Literature I Review*.

CONTENTS

Part I
ISLE OF PROMETHEA

Part II

I AM HEPHAESTUS

Part III

DOUBT

Part IV

MUSTARD SEED

Yea, and if some god shall wreck me in the wine-dark deep,
even so I will endure, with a heart within me patient of affliction.
For already have I suffered full much, and much have I toiled
in perils of waves and war; let this be added to the tale of those.

—Homer, *The Odyssey*, Book V

Part I
ISLE OF PROMETHEA

INVOKING ERATO
for Audre Lorde

    Won't you help me?
I'm awash in words, arms tired, sore.
    Won't you help me
bail the words? Writing is rough sea;
I'm lost, foundering without oars;
perched on the thwart, I drift offshore.
    Won't you help me?

LADY TIRESIAS: SEVEN YEARS A WOMAN

No form will do for this work. Augury is simply a job
to be done. I sit with head lowered, an unthreatening figure
at the well. Though blind, I can read the meaning in all lives
save my own. I know the meaning of the signs: the scorched
ivy climbing the courtyard wall, the rusting hasp
meant to hold the run-down gate, the virgin's furtive glance,
the snakes intertwined. No relief comes
at night. The first time I lay with a man I understood
the importance of whether a woman offers you her mouth or not.
A woman may offer what lies hidden below, but never that
which rises above: her heart, her hands, her lips, her mind.
By day, the crowds wait and wait and wait amid detritus, disease.
The lines do not let up. Some dreaming of floods, others dreaming
of easier work, the laborers patiently cue around, a braid
amid the prostitutes, the money-lenders, the fishmongers
for the one truth they already know. For it is always the same
utterance I offer: *An empty bed can rule your mind like fire.*
I am a foreigner to this body, and no one will dare break
bread with me because the small-talk never comes easy.

PENELOPE'S WEB

Catholic, we stood at the back of First Missionary
Baptist. Tears heavy as oil, committed and uncommitted
to the crossroads Fortune had laid like mercy

before us. The black limousine an omen,
having broken down as my father and I lurched
over the one respectable hill in Harrison County.

Before that mishap, Mama and I abandoned the rituals of
hair and nails, a pair of klepto-nymphs ripping
tender limbs of flesh-white magnolias before dawn.

Homage to rain: Daddy, like always, devoid of tact,
said exactly what he meant. "You don't have to
do this." The gown half-done, I barely whip-

stitched in, for I had been sewing and unsewing
seeded pearls all night. Quite aware of my past, my kin
placed exotic bets about how long Spring might last.

Little girls do marry their fathers. Icarus
could not help but see himself in Ulysses,
the selfish pride of the barrel chest at the other

end of the aisle. No comparison here. The organ cried
a chorus, wild sadistic pleasure at my going. Drylongso!
Who knew that Ulysses would spend my youth

thus. My heels punched their way through
the cheap crumple of white paper. Rose petals signified
blood. I was torn, wishing no parts of either world.

SISYPHUS

Pick the clothes up
off the floor. Empty and clean
the diaper pail. Laundry. Light, dark.
Pick and sort. Oh yeah, don't
forget—brush your teeth. Unload
the dishwasher. Take out the trash.
Make groceries. You have to eat. Not
this way, that way. Not that way, this.
Wash the tub out. Change the toilet
paper. So much for glamour. Get up
at four to dress for work. Meeting
after useless meeting. Grade
the papers, mark the texts. Answer
the phone. *Yessuh. Yessuh*
"Yes, sir. No, sir—I can't
stay late again." Ride the train
for yet another unending hour.
Traffic seems like a gift from heaven,
mindless minutes all to myself.
Get off the train at five, be home by six.
Keep moving. Push. Don't you even
think about being tired. Phone call.
"Could you? Can you please?"
"No, I can't." *Dialtone.*
Drone. Trudge to the kitchen,
fix the food, do the dishes,
scrub the scuff marks off the floor.
This is what passes for exercise.
By the way, don't forget . . .

Wash your ass. Bathe the babies.
Breathe.
Make love and fall asleep. Then,
pick the clothes up . . . .

THE ACHILLES POEM: HEEL

When the call heralds over the rough stone fence,
attempt to feign these words: *resignation, duty.*
Inside, know that you revel in escaping

the tedium. Being clean, quiet, orderly. Mending
all the objects and psyches you didn't break,
the delicate math of bartering for what

you want. How, by day's end, the woman you love
has no energy left for desire. You think, *This is
not a man's life. This is not how a man lives.*

Yet, one cannot deny she was the hearth you quested.
As you dress, remain silent, apart. Do not make excuses
about your leaving. *She will know. She has always*

known the way you strategically eye each battle,
knowing there is nothing to lose: not mortality,
not homestead, not pain. Nothing. Fighting beyond

endurance is the marrow of a man's life. Envision yourself
striding over a field of stones and dirt, slaying slaves and
children fool enough to believe they want to become men.

You are the fearful shadow imprinted upon the iris of another
man's soul. You are myth, not mythology. The sword without
actual need of shield, the sweet tender spot aching.

ICARUS

I don't care if glue and wax won't hold
the feathers long. A pale moon shares

this morning with the sun. I remember
all my father's misshapen admonitions.

I've watched him buckle beneath his fears,
living in this world. Pain blossoms

like betrayals from my shoulder blades.
Gravity is always calling, calling. Soaring

through clouds as my gaze seeks the ground,
I watch the mortals push their crumbs,

their empty gestures. I envy their ability
to pretend at satisfaction. I realize I am

no more than a winged animal seeking
glory. The gods look down from above,

pity me, offer me this one gift. A trance.
The sun beckons, offering its testimony.

With hunger and aerial tricks, the body
fools the mind. Glide, whirl, climb higher.

Always seek the pattern. I am a simple man
willing to risk one wistful kiss upon the sea.

CHARON THE FERRYMAN

There's always somebody striking up a song. Off-key.
Wade in the Waters usually be the one, forcing me
to paddle back through the mud and sand,
mid-crossing, to drive back the shades.

I don't have time for customers who can't pay.
Everybody's always looking for the hook-up.
For a one-way trip, I only charge them
one lousy coin. I don't think it's too much

to ask. But my clientele thinks differently. They are
worse than little kids waiting the long hour
after they eat to slide back into the pool. Only this
ain't no regular hour, if you've been waiting

long as most of them have. An hour can seem like
a hundred years, so a hundred years must seem
long as hell. Then there are the hotheads, the ones
who want to argue the meaning of "proper." What e*xactly,*

they say, is "proper?" What it *supposed* to look like. And what
dicty person made up some rules for *my* burial? They roll their
                    eyes,
swivel their long necks. Anybody with that kind of time on their
                    hands
must not be getting any at home. Ain't got anything better to do

than think up ways to make *my* death more miserable.
Can I see a copy of these here rules? Let me talk
to the man in charge. I try to tell them how
Hades is a mighty wealthy man, explain

that he's too busy to deal with their kind
of nonsense. That's when they get personal. Making fun
of my boat, ragging on my clothes. How
they didn't want to ride in no rustbucket no how.

That they would never be caught dead
with somebody who has to cinch his clothes up
in knots. For somebody who makes as much
as he does off us (They talk like I'm not even there.)

you'd think he'd dress better—and get himself a shave.

PARIS

My mama named me Paris
because it was a world of lights and language
she'd never see or use. DC, born and raised,
Mama ain't never been farther than Vienna,

end of the Orange Line,
where she scrubbed floors for a pasty woman who
set aside a separate plate, fork, and glass
special, for you and who,

try as she might,
would never be
any kind of close, family friend. Too much
history is the simplest version of this particular

lie. I'm Southeast. I deals
a little of this, a little of that,
tries to be a good shepherd
to my flock. Look out for the

women of my runners. Watch as
they mamas and sisters get off
the bus at the corner. We all watching,
we make sure they get home

safe. Once Lady Jones asked us to look and see
if we could fix her
busted motion light. A stray bullet. I shoulda known
her friends fingered me as the soft touch.

I gotta quit those 'Bama pleasantries,
always sayin' *please* and *thank you*. *Ma'am* and *Sir*.
I shoulda known. There was gonna be
some shit.

Me an Jupe went on around
there to find three females,
way past anybody's lap dance,
they asses and they mouths

swinging back-forth, forth-back. Real sly,
they asked Jupe
"Who asked look-ed best? Which one
still gots the stuff to make

a grown man cry?" Jupe bent over
scooped up his tools, said that
he'd be seein' me.
So the question naturally

falls in my lap. They slid, half-slide
their sweaty palms across thick, polyester thighs,
made me all kinds of promises they got
no business

makin'. That's how it is
with them old-timey women. They
mean well but
can't never deliver.

HERA HAS HER SAY

Ours is a gin town full of relations.
My husband and I are prominent citizens
here. The way we love each other smacks
of incest. My father and mother
were brother and sister. My husband and I
are brother and sister. Like most Southern towns,
scandals are common. People need
clear definitions of good and evil.
For the sake of convenience, I have been
assigned the latter.
                          The women here
admire my beauty, though they persist in describing
me as matronly. When I slip on my voile sundress,
I can still hold my own with any of these young
things. I know it's the contradictions that keep
a man's attention. These nubile girls
still locked under they daddy's roof have difficulty
understanding such a concept. See, it's natural
for one to believe, especially when one is still young,
that youth is beautiful in itself. They forget
youth is everywhere for the taking. Men find it
puzzling, they don't understand their own
fascination with me. My raven mane reflects
grass and skies like the iridescent eyes of a peacock's plume.
My pale arms and bovine stare contradict
what's hinted at beneath the thin cotton. This show of skin
 (light, bright) they take for proof that the rest of me has never
been touched . . . A prize denied to even the Sun is surely
worth coveting. My wide brown gaze loses something

15

in translation. All of this can't be
reconciled with my décolletage,
which grown men seem to view
only in terms of sex.

I wedded

early. Folks around here use my marriage
as other towns would use a statue. Historical record,
landmark, a visual point of reference for giving
directions to people passing on their way through to
some place else. In exchange for this stability, people seek
our advice just because we haven't killed
one another.

My man Z got one of them roving eyes.

Churchgoers and heathen alike admire him
for it. His stutter talk followed by the pickup's
roar into a cloud of smoke always means he's slipped
off to get his buckle shined.

The sight of him

speeding off to see someone else, the same way
he used to speed off to see her, killed
one little girl who thought she was in love.
One time I caught him lowriding a white Caddy.
Shameful. A man old as he is,
all slunk down, near falling over in the seat.
One hand barely on the wheel, the other elbow
jutting cross the armrest. I threw
my arms around him, kissed and cooed
like he had bought the car for me. I drove
all over town, told every gossip I could find, even paid

a visit to the woman it belonged to. I know,
every time she hears my name,
surely it feels like a gadfly biting her ass.

IAGO'S LAMENT

There are far too many Iagos in the world.
So why am I here swiveling my body,
stoked, fighting off the grave? I crave sleep
the way an abused child seeks intervention.

I had no patience for Desdemona & Othello.
Such a ragged way to be taken down. To be so
virtuous, so, so *pure*. Give me some dirt, I'll create
a masterpiece! It's far more heady to run with jackals,

pick the city streets clean, to be a bum sucking
marrow from the bone, to gnash gristle to bits,
content to lick my haunches and howl. But then
there remains a certain risk of being . . .

slapdash. I mean, creating torment for the masses
requires unflagging discipline, and I've searched out that
exquisite wrench of pain, that inescapable need to be
upended and devoured—by your own. Kind.

ISMENE SPEAKS

Eteocles and Polynices are dead.
Haemon and Eurydice are dead.
My sister escaped being buried alive
only to become strange fruit.

May Thebes gather rotting figs and make
bittersweet wine. Antigone, I call your name.

I told her that the dead really don't so much mind
vultures and dogs. I pulled her close, whispered bromides,
how a long life, well-lived, is revenge enough.

But any woman who tries to outdo a blind man in his blindness
will never satisfy herself with dropping tears upon silt,
an open grave. No matter, I still broke fool and tried to swallow
a lie. For all my efforts, she just wished me

dead. Piteous, her form. Flailing between earth and sky,
a statue in the dust. A woman wailing, striking her breasts.

I hope you don't plan to lecture me.
About patriarchy, about kissing the rod.
About benevolent, white father figures.

I know all about uncles who rend your world
and grudgingly offer you needle and thread.

E TRUE HOLLYWOOD STORY: M—

I only said that we looked
about the same size. How was I to know
that an off-hand remark
would be regarded
like Friday's catch served fresh Monday.
Okay, maybe I did *kinda-sorta-perhaps*
happen to have mentioned
that some of her tracks might need some more
glue. That sister/girl thing is a tenuous
business at best, but any real woman knows
her hair—today—is her
only crowning glory. So I've always kept
my hair done and my sisters as
my only counsel. They actually seem to appreciate
my jokes.
                    Minerva's sibilant campaign
began thus. Planting lies, lies, nothing but lies.
Everyone knew she was eye-twitching
three-hundred-sixty-five-days-a-year
crazy. She even sent a known busybody to do
her dirt. My every utterance
misconstrued, slip-sliding free of
my good intentions. My good name
swallowed whole. This is how
living gets to be so tedious. This is why
people turn to stone.

MINOTAUR'S CODA

I have had my children steal away Athens' sacred scrolls
feting King Aegeus and King Theseus, and I must call
bullshit. You enlisted your indentured scribes and lied,
positing the City's glorious amnesia as truth, as history.
One must question a king who abandons his child.
However, leaving your wife is simply an old story
unworthy of mention. Why not say what we know:
Raising children, being monogamous is just hard, plain

hard. Points which I will concede for I was not there:
the moving of the stone, the finding of the sword.
Even of Sinis and Sciron, I cannot claim to know
anything of anyone else's childhood. Half-bull, half-
man, I can only say that children are mean little adults
in training. (They used to say my father fucked a fat cow.)

Yet, a pact had been made. Aegeus and Minos had
no interest in, no patience for the day-to-day
raising of children. Tired of all the backtalk,
the dishes and chalices left about the palace. Apocrypha
hints that Minos was actually overheard saying he wanted
nothing more than his ingrate of a son dead.

Aegeus let his inner circle know that for a small *tribute*
every nine years, he could rid them of fourteen
troublesome daughters and sons, and their parents could brag
how their children attended an elite boarding school in Crete.

21

A maze: Something inside me desires hunger and courts
emptiness. If I have anything left to offer after fostering
generation after generation of children, it is this. My unbidden
palm outstretched. The way certain minds freed of time can
follow Ariadne's golden thread, expand and excise maps
leading back to anything that may have once been called a life.

No, Ariadne did not leave. She did not die. Although
when Theseus sailed away—without her—she wanted to.
Her fate had been made clear. Slow affection. All those
backwaters, all those nervous tributaries, all those walls
represented her yearning to float away free. Strange,
have you ever seen how the bowed limbs of red yucca
arc against the blue sky like blood on water? Mine,

yours. Even our most surreal dreams are rooted
in reality. Whether myth or legend, somehow
Ariadne and I managed to hack ourselves free.

ECHO ON A GOOD DAY

Most days are like this one,
dark, dank. A guttering candle
my only light. I work on perfecting—
a better word would be practicing,
my smile. That, I know, is what
startled Narcissus. The way my incisors
catch
       the apple of my bottom lip
drawing two neat drops of blood.

       Everyone wants Narcissus.
       Men, women. That also
       adds to this quandary.

I haven't spoken today.
Not much
       worth repeating anymore.
This is a typical day for me,
full of loneliness.
       In my mind
I practice two of the three words
I will say. *Come* _____ *me.*
Only the preposition causes trouble.
On different days, I am sure I know
the one I mean: *to, for, in, on.*

       Redoubtable is love,
       especially this one that uses
       hearts as whetstones.

Books cover the walls, the floor, my bed
like dross. I lie prone
hours, barely moving.
Plundering gracile words
I will repeat
              as if my own. My voice
runs breathless circles in my throat,
desperate to enter my mouth. Appetent,
my tongue tells my ears
dulcet tales of what awaits.

  Pain is more bearable
  when you have something
  beautiful as a distraction.

When I've been diligent, I reward myself
with goblets of wine. Alcohol goes
straight to my sex. Engenders a bloom
of purple, a lissome reminder of my beloved.

LEDA TO HER YOUNGER SELF

You gave yourself willingly after you saw
snow drift through an arc of light and mist
like souls to dark earth without shame.
This memento mori became the bent cage
that set you free. Soon, you will find that
the stone in your chest will also become a comfort:

Desire loves what it wants without reason. Faithless,
you will forget your other younger selves, the ones who
followed rules. Try not to be afraid. Who you once were
is gone. Leda, you will remember feathers against skin,
acts that had no name. Joy in bas relief, painting
songs without slumber. Yes, bliss once spoke your name.

One day soon, you will begin to waste
slow hours watching the horizon, cradling four children,
yearning for any hint of pearlescent water and sky
as you dream of the only fire that soothes.
You will swear each remembrance of that day
your last—as the swan, once again, extends its wings.

NIOBE

I couldn't stand there another second.
There they were, lauding
a woman who had had only two babies.

That's how I ended up with—fourteen.
Women lie to one another. Don't cut
one another

the teensiest bit of slack. So, here I am
back up, again, kissing yet another
morning that shouldn't have my name

on it. Making bottles and changing sheets
will take the better part of the day.
And I will, of course, be sleep come noon.

My man brought me
the baby at 1 AM. I was up
frantically trying to read, trying to write.

The time nobody else wants
is the only time I can call
my own. I've already picked out

a black dress. Because, like me, my babies trust
too much. I mark time, packing lunches, signing
progress reports, listening for the whistle of arrows.

PERSEPHONE: ALL BOUND UP

I had been gone days before my mother noticed.
Demeter, so busy with the exigencies of living
had not guessed I'd gone. Gone. No grip,
no valise, just my weakened determination
to find a plausible escape from Zeus, that arse.
For this reason, I do not embellish doors
deadbolted, nor thighs grazing across window sills.
All that pretense, just for show. I merely traipsed after
a thought, for if I could scramble after that thought,
any thought, my mind would not collapse upon itself.

Begin here: Let Hades off the hook. Irons fashioned
into curved points are not conducive to truth-telling.
Isn't every marriage an abduction? (Stop,
insert archaic smile.) No, I let him wear me down,
for there are so few men deserving of women
like me, epic landscapes who consider being anyone's
queen a burden, robe or no robe. Certainly, he knew
I could have survived on rue tea several months
more. But the world needed a silvered-veined leaf,
a yarn capable of dividing boredom into
recognizable seasons. Alas, poor Hades.
Six pomegranate seeds? Mythology's rube.

Helios swears he surveys all. Okay, he does, but why
did he decide upon such a fanciful lie. Abduction? Me,
come now. Tsk, tsk. No one would be so foolish.
He had observed I only brought the most
well-behaved songbirds home, guided them carefully

through the rituals, then wrung each neck. He read
the signs: A mother desires normalcy for her daughter.
Rape, however unimaginable, proved a more suitable lie.

Dead, I watch the cardinal attack its glass image
each morning, then alight upon the day and am always
reduced to tears. This is what I miss most: dawn
in my mother's house. I should have known,
I certainly should have known. Having lain with Zeus
like a statue with dead eyes, Mama would've understood.

ISLE OF PROMETHEA

I am being killed by what keeps me from dying.
—Hélène Cixous, *The Book of Promethea*

No wily mind do I possess. For if I did,
would I be chained, thus, to this rock, with lengths
of metal, grey like my mind and just as stolid? These manacles
bruise what joy I might hope to find and the sound of my own
bondage shakes me free of intermittent sleep. Daybreak.
          Unbidden,
the eagle, as if by prayer, cuts the sky, all beak and talons
focused upon my flesh. I half-smile and nod assent, impart
a blessing for his sake that he even bothers to remember
to visit me each day. A poor host, I can only offer
my liver, white with lust, a sweetbread I can't give away.
So, I am accused of stealing fire. Explain the sense of stealing
what no one wants anyway. Look carefully at me, the way I am,
bound, hardwired to the bifurcated desires this body demands.
The thunder, and the thunder, and the thunder sounds.
Pedestrian, I have never managed to outrun the lightning.
I find solace in this rock, surrounded by a wake of water and sky
abandoned by Zeus without benefit of even a copse of trees
to contemplate in the gloaming. Left alone again, I stir
the embers of what I could never steal, for the fire was always,
and ever will be, mine to do with as I please.

HOW OFTEN IN DARKNESS

I. Venus
You will not believe
that anything from a womb sacred as mine
would have anything to do
with someone like her. But he did. So I aimed at keeping
him from her. I never understood what he wanted
with a shameless hussy like that. She was
incapable of goodness. While the women-
folk cooked, she would take her stand
among the men. For this reason alone,
those fools worshipped her
more than me. It didn't take a genius to know
this would simply never do.

I saw how the heat softened the streets to make her
walking easy. I saw
women offer her friendship
like their best sun-ripened mangoes.
Man goes. I saw the way
that ingrate dropped each green-red fruit in her sack.
Heaven only knows what she did with them.

What does a woman, hard and dark
like the pits of such sweet gifts
have need of any man, much less my son?

II. Cupid

When I met her, my mama didn't think I knew
the mind of this woman
who would become my wife.
I saw her for what she was. Who wouldn't recognize
skid marks on white cotton?

Her eccentricities filled me
like shame. I had to have her. No matter
that the purple and yellow pansies in her hair would later become
a reason to hate her. No matter that she welcomed
me to her to her bed without even knowing my name.
No matter that her beloved sisters slid
their soft-lined palms across my crotch
every chance they got. From the start, I knew
I had no more chance of making an honest woman of her
than I had of controlling the zephyr
that brought her to me.

But who knew that she was capable of stabbing
a burn through my heart?

III. Psyche

Shame is the one gift that he gave me that
did not have some demand attached.

How often in darkness—undressing,
our backs to one another—we did without light.
Cautiously, timidly I tiptoed while fear turned the knife
concerning that awkward, subjective pronoun
us. I learned to hone my words.

31

Whole conversations became stabs
at understanding how long I was expected
to wander, seeking the approval of a woman
who would never forgive me for giving
her son the one thing
she could not? Each night, her boy came
to me. Love expected me to ask no questions
of where he'd been all day. All night
I traced the outline of my life on the ceiling as I listened
while he snored. L egs straight, hands by my sides.
I would lie perfectly still.
Locked within myself, I labored for hours,
trying to match my breath to his.

I had no other choice. I turned to prayer.
When that failed
I resorted to novenas. The result was always the same:
a scratchy voice and sore knees.

What was I supposed to do? Each night
I asked myself how long was long enough. How long
must one sleep, side-by-side,
on a sickbed of emptiness.

Living with him like that, I moved beyond
the need for tangibles. I finally swallowed
all the questions I did not ask. They shaped
my spine into a scythe.

A Siren Repents

These conversations with my past make me know
I loathe frailty in others because I hate it in myself.
I don't mean to keep you. I will let you go

back to your habit of castaway loves. There are those,
stones and oceans, that bespeak loss and meeting. Lifetimes of
these conversations with the past make me know

that re/memory, like film, disintegrates, dissolves with no
permanence at all. I swore to myself I'd keep this brief.
I didn't mean to keep you. I will let you go.

Some words can exist without being spoken, but do you
ever whisper my name? I do yours. It catches my throat like
                    grief,
and these conversations with my past are all that make me know.

Please leave me something—more than sad lyrics of woe . . .
Because I have known you, I have had to become more aloof,
but I don't mean to keep you, I will let you go.

Sometimes between stones and oceans—former friends, now
                    foes
—there can exist a stretch of light, sweet oblivion beyond belief.
These conversations with the past are what make me know
I never could have kept you. I had to let you go.

EURIDICE

It is hard to make your way back
from the Underworld with two good legs,
and here I am doing my best to follow after,
my ankle being what it is, nearly lame. I lag behind,

further and farther, hoping he will find comfort
in the *thump-drag* rhythm of things to come.
He is singing a song I don't know, in an octave
my voice only dreams of, so I hum to hold back

the pain. I watch the light bend and break
around the open spaces. Between the meat of his arm and his
                    chest,
between the back of his knees and his behind. We have come
this far by faith. One more obstacle. We must ford

Lethe, the river of forgetting. My feet test the sharpness of each
rock. I must not fail him. The water is so much colder
than I recall. My teeth grit, I fix my gaze
upon his back. The lyre he holds above his head like a sacrifice

to the vulgar ochres of the sky. The lives of the dead
float their way toward me. My hair fans the water's surface, a
                    seine,
a remembrance of hell. The water rises, thigh to hip to
                    stomach,
still higher, until the river clasps her wet fingers around my
                    throat,

34

tickles me beneath my chin. I press my lips tight and quit
moaning just long enough to take
one last deep breath. Nothing but the sound of rushing water
remains. Orpheus cannot help himself. He looks back.

GOD FORBID: KING SALMONEUS

I've been talking to God.
He refuses to talk back. Thus, I decided
to steal Zeus's thunder, have my
stable boy harness my four best
prized horses. Brash, wild. Using hemp
ropes I rigged kettles and cymbals to my chariot,
built a bronze bridge of sound to reach across,
on up through apathy. A person can wait forever
seeking rapture. I made
the effort, though *my* father had warned
. . . about "the perils of lopsided
relationships." Yes, yes. I wanted
to be Zeus. Honored, worshipped,
desired. Not another
lowly king ending domestic squabbles
over swine and plots of land, not a man
hated by his own brother. Mortal, I am.
We all are.
                     One's wife dies. Out of habit,
a middle-aged man may take
another, but this new one might just
hate your daughter. Such is life. So you
turn away from living,
dream of heresy, harness your imagination
to sound: the word, the image.
What of impiety. One may nod,
demanding *hello* of all and any passersby.
(Even if they only walk faster and cast their
resentments toward the ground.)

If only once, one must risk
raising a splayed palm to shade one's eyes
and look directly into the sun.

I felt the thunder before I saw the light.

Inescapable, some landscapes must be set
on fire. So, here I am among the Titans,
and Tartarus looks a lot like the suburbs.
Amazingly, beneath heaven and earth,
here, in this hell, I have salvaged peace.

Part II
I AM HEPHAESTUS

I.

My parents are quite literally gods.
    Abnormally beautiful and self-
absorbed. And like all beautiful,
self-absorbed women and men who make the
mistake of marrying one another, they have
faults. Plural, possessive.
(I must take my time. Go slow.)
First,
    although they married
each other, they always thought they could do
better. You know. Someone
taller, perhaps, with straighter
teeth and better opportunities. Next,
    the only opinion that ever really
mattered to them
is how they would fare in a rival's estimation.
Then,
    the one that explains this
laying bare
of family business is this. The only reason my
mother had children was because
she desired
proof, some life-size tangible to
remind her how
sublime she once was. Finally,
    everything I've said, am
saying, will say
is
harsh but true. Harsh. But
so true.

II.

Sometimes, like now, the best place to start is
the beginning, but where is that?
How does one get there?

III.

The woman who gave birth to
me
            (I suppose some might hazard the word *mother*)
had a difficult time. The pain must have been enough
to make her delusional, for she swears
I came from her thigh. This is nothing unusual
in the way of history
below the Mason-Dixon. The façade
is always more important than what's underneath.
Consider this. Not one, but two
parents who've made a point
of not remembering
their children's birthdays. No months, no days. Zounds,
        they can't even keep straight
who was born, much less who was born when
and in what order.
Another testament to
the power of the vain to shroud
the scandalous.
                My father
says he gave birth to my sister Athena
and that I helped. All this
from the top of his head. No, not that one, the
unimaginative one
on the top of his neck. And not to be outdone, the

42

woman biologically responsible for my being
insists on believing she bore me to spite
my father, that I was
immaculately conceived. Of course,
she uses the term *parthenogenetically*.
(I wonder if that's anything like in vitro.)

IV.
So, blood is spewing forth like lava and
what limps forth but a squat, hirsute
thick-necked
boy with two clubbed feet.
Needless to say that the woman
who claims to be my mother isn't
pleased. Immediately
she thinks my father will point an
iron finger at her side
of the gene pool. She forgets the gothic
bent of what it means to be Southern
(Our family tree has no branches.)
and promptly tosses me over
the balcony, the proverbial
baby with the bath water.
Everyone has a crazy relative or three.
But this nut cleans herself up,
powders her nose, and goes out
for the evening to play bid whist and tell gossipy
anecdotes about cheating husbands and ugly babies with
those adders
she calls friends.
                    Around these parts people

say that if your daddy
don't claim you can "get in line,"
but if your mama don't want you,
"you're messed up for life." I suspect that
that's true,
                        because much-too-much later
I thought about
paying money to consult a
psychoanalyst,
but my parents said that sort of foolishness
was for mortals. All I know is the
greatest falls always happen just
beyond your mother's sight and,
no matter how sincere
the remorse, the regret—
later, if it comes is
quite useless
once the damage is done.

V.
I fell past self-loathing, past
despair,
into the depths of self-pity,
landing utterly
broken.
Two kindly ladies were good enough to
take me in. I was in a bad way.
Papa, a rolling stone. Mama masquerading as
an upstanding woman in the community.
Rock and a fucked place
if ever there was one.

44

Not to mention, enough bastard
brothers and sisters to keep
a probate lawyer in work for life.
Don't think I don't have
an appreciation for small miracles.
What else can you call it
when a woman with three fair-cheeked daughters—a
bounty of splendor,
mirth and cheer—
takes in a no-name boy who falls
whence the gods only know.
By anybody's open-ended clock,
nine years is a longish time
to clothe and feed
the most obliging of visitors,
to say nothing of a gimp who
sets up
a forge
smack-dab in
the middle
of your living room.
I can't imagine what she
told her husband. Or
where she got it all.
Hammer, anvil, tongs.
Whatever I needed
Eurynome and her friend Thetis
brought.

VI.

I made them gifts. They suffered
my first shabby attempts with smiles. Combs
with crooked teeth,
brooches that wouldn't close, corsets
that bruised. They accepted all I
gave. The harmony
of Eurynome's daughters,
such voices surging and waning
alongside the hydro twang of my Art
somehow made the scintillating
fires less intense,
made my past seem
 almost irrelevant. I
fell
in love with them all. How could one
not?

　　　And her daughter Aglaia became the
wife of my youth.

　　　　　　But what did we know
of husbandry. Some things are better left
unlearned. My work was my mistress.
Her sisters were her life. When we parted, we
parted
friends. No hard feelings, no
bitter words.

VII.

One day, very very early,
before Eurynome's morning bath,
before I could drag myself upright, my

brother Dodo shows up drunk, saying
Ma and Pa want me
home.
He's ogling
the rising beauties.
I cringe. He's pawing Ocean's
tapestry.
Oh, let me die of shame!
Needless to say, this is not the way
I imagined the heralding of my homecoming. No
pomp, no circumstance,
no teary apologies
flowing into cups of mead.
Just a dipsomaniacal brother
talking loud, disrespecting the
hearth of the woman
who gave me her daughter's hand,
and bore me no ill will for
my failure.
Eurynome
closed her mind
to whatever else might come. She
spoke simply.
"We are merely your family,
they are your blood.
We will always be here, a womb to
which you can return.
About them,
I can make no such promises."

VIII.

I return.
My mother pretends to fawn,
my father boasts.
Patronizing
the likes of which
the gods have never seen. Both
promise that I'll make everything
for everyone.
"No problem at all" . . .
they say,
without ever having consulted
me. They never paused to consider that
I'm a grown man,
that I might have plans of my own, that
I may have no wish to make
trinkets and thunderbolts, unbreakable
locks,
golden armor and golden beds, scepters,
thrones, chariots, homes, spears, bows,
sickles,
an aegis and,
get this, a
woman!
I didn't even ask
What for?
          No one ever said, "Let
me pay you for your time?" No
one ever said,
"What supplies do you require?"
No one ever said,

"May I keep you
company while you work?"
Their only concern was
"When will it be ready?
And how come it takes
so damn long?"
So here I am and they're acting as
if I'm the faithful retainer returned
to the Big House,
the new nigger in Olympus, the
only one with a job.

IX.
I will not be the keeper of secrets.

X.
Everyone calls me Baby Hugh or
Hef. My dad's the playboy, not
me. The irony isn't wasted.
People always wonder aloud
about an august man
with an ugly woman.
Apropro, the reverse is not
true. Aphrodite
became wife number two. Women
have this ability to overlook
appearances when Love
is involved. I'm sure some thought
Poor dear while others envisioned
elaborate scenes of rape. coersion
and mind control, reinforced

chains and engorged instruments.
But there was
nothing quite so barbarous.
Only my unwitting adoration
of a woman
—Confound her soul!— who
on the surface appeared to be
my better. And there were
whole weeks
when the vicissitudes of our life
together seemed almost
normal.
She would attend my shoulders,
salve my burns. I would untangle,
brush, and braid
her hair. I learned never
to speak
of the knots, the liaisons
my hand could not undo,
for then she would
lock her door to me.
Each time, I would cry
like a howling wind
caressing a closed window,
trying to remember a
better use for pain.

XI.

There was no invisible net,
save for Aphrodite's guilty conscience.

The sun shone on two bodies
warring toward bliss. Neither
of which was mine.

There was no fettered throne,
just powerlessness.

My mother never wrestled against
the trappings of second-hand glory,
yet my successes were poison to her soul.

Such stories began as all myths do,
someone spinning sugar and hot air to
make implausible lies sound blue.

I never demanded apologies.
I simply wanted
for either Aphrodite or Hera to speak
the reality of what was.
But what I need, I logically know neither
can give.

XII.

Do I understand Hera better now? I
want to say I do.
The embarrassment, the casting aside.
I know both these sentiments
intimately. Because an artisan plans
such elaborate dreams
as fools dare not even hope;

51

he delights beneath the heft
of what cannot be controlled.

(An uneasy peace conceals
many a ravaged heart.)

Sometimes our creations
put to shame our crude imaginings.

Sometimes our children are beasts, quite
horribly not what we intend.

Part III

DOUBT

DARK SORROWING

God knows the burdened soul's dark sorrowing
When hearts are sadly pregnant with old fears.
— James Seamon Cotter, Jr., "Sonnet XVI"

I.

I have walked miles for nothing
for less than nothing, past the church
slanting and sloping from both
dilapidation and song.

This is a bedroom
community set below the watertable,
a sandy square dotted with sparse oases—
tufts of culture, the occasional mirage.

Shotgun shanties crouch low among
the weeds, shouldered between a
trailer park and a ravine beneath a
mackerel sky.

II.

I have walked the distance and am tired
of people—including myself. The way
they pare away at the taut folds of flesh
with the chinked, rusted accoutrements of
dolts. Perhaps I am
a misanthrope. I lament that
those without sin should cast
the first stone as I go on

55

yammering through these forays
into the ascetic recesses of my mind.

I inhale the coarseness of the milieu.
I hear a smiler say, *Well, go on, man,
hit the bitch.* I know I am doomed.

III.

I have walked while fever gnashed at my mind. Having
been so much to so many for so long,
I long to be nothing to anyone now. I return
home and lower the blackout curtains
against the workaday sun. I feel the dampness, a
syrupy mix—an augur of lavender and mold.

The wallpaper curls like the sable lashes of
a newborn. This place is where I begin the
ritual. I kilt the black shroud
up over the corners, over the patina, over
the heavy gilt
that adorns the concaved
mirror, to witness the shadowy still life
meticulously arranged into a demure mural where
the distinctions between
may and *can* are observed
with the diligence of the faithful.

I speak the word aloud. *Pray.*
I break this monosyllable over coffee as

easily I break
bread at the sideboard.

IV.

I have walked all this way,
and there is a point to this: My anger, my
alarum is real, not disinterested.

I am trying to reify
what some say does
not exist. Imagine . . .

The sacrificial lamb—knees vaselined,
not against ash, but against cracking
—a girl child praying beneath the hands of
a blind man with congealed, dead eyes.
A priest who will never see her until
the cataract of religion is removed.

 See, like a moll, I am intimate
with concepts I cannot begin to construct.

V.

I have walked miles for this, specifically to
dial 411 and request the listing
of the Man in the Moon. I figure
surely, if God has allowed anyone,
any pagan that is, amid his cronies
a hermit with a crater face
would not be a threat to such an ego.

There is no answer, so I write myself
letters of grace like John's epistles.
I become forlorn when I realize
there will be no reply. It is at these
moments in which fate reveals
the bedevilment of living. I see
that even if, by chance,
the rapture sought me out, found its way down around
the league of curtains and down
the straightshot of the warped floorplanks
to descry my form, it could not vivisection
my whole
into perfect parts. Only martyrs
die for faith. I am but a pagan,
though in a trance, yet I am just
catholic enough for the circus maximus.

VI.

I have walked miles searching for Grace.

In the beginning was the word . . . .
I do believe the question
of the chicken or the egg
simpler for a mind such as mine.

My mind is maimed, withered by atrophy, slumped
to one side, drooling
in a steel contraption meant to afford autonomy.

Like a quadriplegic, I am left with sufferances, procuring
favors from one who sent

a child—the literal embodiment of Truth and Grace—
to be food and drink for cannibals.

Truth does not necessarily set you free, but it can make
life tolerable, so I am reduced to
making deals with God.

One day the rain sounds like applause and
you're brazen enough to
give anybody some lip. Hell,
so bold as to tell an outright lie,
staring straight ahead, without blinking.

Breckinridge Mill Dam: Virginian Summer

. . . The place was shown to be very like the last time. A piece was not exchanged, not a bit of it, a piece was left over. The rest was mismanaged.

—Gertrude Stein, "A Frightful Release"

Victorian, how you fall like water
for gravity and anything else that pulls you down,
claiming chaos—your natural state.
In Steinese, a dam is a dam is a dam. But is it? Am I?

You descend in angry fluvials—blind rapids
determined to find entrance to pumice-grey
stones devoid of all mortal sensations; the rocks you choose:
of Gibraltar, of Ages, Stonehenge, any, any, any

hobby-store quartz or common fossilized stone. Smashed-faced
water sprites skim your surface then cling
like white-knuckled vines suckered to your back—a tight
eddying habit. You have no desire. You kick, bite, scratch,

fight as you course through my fingers stretched wide as
                    floodgates,
enraged that I make no effort to catch you. I will not, I shall not.
As minnows dart between my toes, I strip to midwaist and dive
away, exposing more of myself than you can bear.

SALT

In a trice, I am made whole. Here
you are, a brigand lying in wait,
circumspect amid a brown study, waiting

to be fulfilled. A moment later,
you step forward, close your mouth upon
mine, scoop out my breath

like a wedge of sweet summer melon,
orchestrating a din
within the confines of my chest.

Like madness, you speak in tongues
of rosehips and bright burgundy
apples, of a delicate core of flesh and seed,

of a malleable thorn among nettles—
images shared between your mouth and
mind in an uncertain moment of clarity.

Flushed, you hone your lithe curve
upon me as if I am the fine grit of shingle—
cloven to the last, moist remnant of the sea.

JELLYFISH HEART

She can't do what they do,
can't be who they are. Weeping
willows and creek-
beds fill her brain, backroads
coursing with betrayals
she can't live with or live down.

She needs a special kind of silence,
buckets full of still water. Shale
scooped up and sieved. A memory
can ease a seagull into flight. She
scrapes poverty from underneath
each golden toenail. She's Big Easy and bad

temper all smashed into one.
Without knowing why, that urge moves her
toward an embarrassed gesture
and she tongues the smooth flesh
of her wrist, tasting salt and perfume,
only to understand the sting of the gift,

an absolute certainty, a barometer
measuring what's real and what's false.

THE OBTUSE OF A LITERARY TRIANGLE

*The rawness was hers, not theirs. She could not begin, when
she first met them, to cope with their sophisticated maneuvering
between understood truths and spoken lies.*
                    —Leon Katz, "Introduction" to Gertrude Stein's *Q.E.D.*

Assuming writers   and their work
live separate   lives to be judged,
independent   of each other,
like the haft   of a glint-edged blade,

       explain why the result is not that of a bulb without

       tungsten; why does apodictic light glance

       then plunge like bright knives in the mind?

STAY

I want to feel your daffodils.
A phrase on loan from a prayer,

only one eye shuts. Focuses, then squints.
I fumble the buttons of the tape recorder

lost beneath my clothes. No other words come.
But urgency beckons. I must clasp

my mind around the stroke of each letter
before the emotion begins to drift

away. *I want to feel your daffodils.* Next time,
I trip free of the tub. Mumbling like a lunatic.

My legs, my back. Glistening thoughts.
A conniption of rivers

racing toward the floor. I find pen
but no paper. Then paper, but no ink.

Shake the pen. Curse whatever god
is handy. *I want to feel*

your daffodils. Each time, the words leave you
speechless—like a present you don't deserve.

More reason to believe
that this time is the last. *I want*

to feel your daffodils. This is what it means
to be a servant of breath.

DOUBT

"Blessed are those who don't see, and yet believe."
—John 20:29

I.

This is no walk of faith. Any surety
of step gives him pause. He is now

a silver man with silver hair,
sporting a gently-used navy blue suit,

swinging a cane. An even blue rhythm.
A metronome, a downbeat, a cowbell. On the

one, he eases a heel forward, each step a rebellion.
Slide guitar, a bare ankle above a spectator

prefigures an intersection. Cars, lights, rain.
We all have our own wounds to wade.

Wind the string. Find the chord. Pluck
the tune. There is a steadiness

about him. Carmine and ochre thoughts
toppling the last meters of afternoon light.

II.

He blinks his outrage at remembering
what is no longer there. The bluish-white

beadboards of the rented room. Nicked and bruised,
each slat a spear. Isolation, solace, doubt.

Godhead of memory. He tastes
darkness breaking winter.

III.

The past. Apochrypha. A Virginian
field all aglow. The orange haze

of harvest. A moon-basked heifer,
a country girl of no consequence.

But it was the smell of mown grass,
not the woman. The moon burned his skin

as he traced her dark areolas, the sky
reminding him of the itch

the puritan seed in him said never
to scratch, and yet

he followed her, so she would not
have to go alone.

And walking that faraway mountain
road, like a conversation that thins out

into silence, he searched amongst
the colored gravestones. So many ways of being

67

he could not fathom. He could not imagine
believing in what he could not touch. Her body

above his. And for that one moment
the universe slowed, then stopped

expanding. The angry houselights blinded all reason. Such
                         desperate
faith obscured by felled trees. Lying there, they flickered

their resentment at not being stars. A missionary, a native.
Each possessing a sentiment that might pass for faith.

HER

My pen is a fickle lover. She tells
such stylized lies. "This is not goodbye,

just a temporary parting." "When will you
return?" I ask. She draws

some unintelligible mark upon the page.
"That ain't really none of your business."

Then she says, "Wait for me." So each day
I scrub and preen myself

to a shiny newness for a woman
who may or may not ever

come. She does relish playing
the coquette. I go about arranging

the minutiae upon my desk. Posing myself
how I think she might like me best. Nude,

clothed, or some soporific state of dishabille.
Again, I wait and then wait some more

or play-pretend. Sharpen pencils, reacquaint
myself with my notes. But I never let my mind

wander to whomever else's crotch she might be holding.
I sit, transfixed by the electric white—believing

she will return. Because the day I begin to have
any doubts, I'll have to let her go.

ANNIVERSARY APART

Already I am beginning to forget
how we met. I was a 6th grader
in a capped-sleeved black leotard,
chalked up to my wrists and nursing
a ripped palm. My leather grip
had somehow slid free, and already I had
begun to associate you with pain.

I am already beginning to forget
three summers later. An abandoned
sailboat floating nowhere and the guilt
of latex blood that stained my thighs. Already
I am remembering to forget
that Christmas I came home to be
told about a woman, whose name
I'd never heard and could not pronounce,
had forbidden you to see
me. Begin again, now, and remember
a layover in Atlanta: your twice-broken ankle,
your excuse to come to my job,
and how I took on somebody
else's shift just to summons enough
profanity to shame you. Yes, I am beginning
to remember plane tickets and phone bills
and how you drove down, again and again,
four hours—one way—late Fridays to carry me
back through the darkness
with you—Athens to Charlotte.

Through Winder and Fair Play,
Gaffney and Rock Hill,
Merle Haggard's voice aimed true
sin at us like a static-filled shotgun,
"Today I started Loving You Again,"
all the way there and the rest areas that never
afforded rest—just release. I will never
forget how at my cousin Julia's wedding I said
no damn more and how I called you
motherfucker and *sumbitch*
in front of my strictest aunts, Jackie / Dot,
until I remembered I'd best apologize
(to them, not you). But I will
never forget. Knowing all you knew,
you still showed up at my daddy's door
three months later, you were singing
beautiful nonsense songs in Japanese
as you begged me to listen,
and you said how we both needed
to relent, to accept, to say *yes.*

New York to Atlanta
in Fourteen Hours: 2 AM Conjugal

Highbeams and horns blaring.
Brakelights flare red, then dim.
I rush headlong, a streak

of woman refusing
death, night blindness—a seam
stitched white with wanting. Meek,

made low by bad desire,
I tempt Fate, bet my life,
zigzagging the highway

home to bed him. A wire
of lust heats my blood like
cool, cool junk gone awry.

Vivid

Fireflies adorn
a bank of wild bergamot
to fill a starless, indigo sky.

Your touch awakens
the same magic
and light and clarity.

LUMP OF SUGAR

Your mouth becomes
a smear—
a shocked pink circle—
because I, who won't even
inquire after a late paycheck or
ask for an extra lump of sugar
for my cup of cambric,
am demanding
the most expensive
gift in a voice
clean and hard as ice.

You with yourself.

I am more comely
than I've ever been
before, since, or ever will be
again. Somewhat distant,
in fact. I swivel
a wooden chair, coasters
zooming almost center
of the room, an instant
modern art installation. Quiet
as it's kept, I never back down.
You'll do what you're told. I fold
my arms, turn blue—a brat

cadging your last bit
of hubris, hesitate one moment
more . . . and nod once.

An indication for you to begin.

RED EYE OF DAWN

He's finally gone. I know
I promised I'd quit this habit.

But as his engine turns over, I make sure
his car roars away. Lock the door. Strike

the match. Not a lighter, a wooden match, box-
strike. Light the candle. From the wick,

singe the paper wand. Only one. Quick,
crank the sash. Four turns, not three.

Long honey fingers make artful wings.
A swirling white plume of smoke, a cloud.

Inhale. Hold. Savor. Feel
the limp scrolls of wetness balloon my lungs

into a New England fog. Anxieties billow
out of fleshed grottos, through sheers.

Damn this infernal haze! Self-possession
makes its exodus, takes flight with breath

blazing over rooftops. A steady drizzle
drapes thin as cellophane to reveal stark,

gnarled limbs of green. A tortoiseshell
cat is perched atop a fencepost. I imagine

it doing its dance across the high wire,
shooing a fist of blackbirds.

They leap away into an eternal blue
as my mind lariats the red eye of dawn.

Part IV

MUSTARD SEED

TRYING TO EXPLAIN

Some minds will never grasp the trumpeting
Southern heart. I don't know what to do
without black mountains overflowing with the shouts
and hollers of umpteen mamas calling their children

home. These are my human voices. A purple stream half-
sobbing among the pineywoods, whispering
a rhapsody like glory pure. I miss common folks
who ain't too shame to dance

an all-embracing reverie to the blues.
I want to be back where the saved and the damned reside
side-by-side and are oft times one and the same.
I'm homesick for gossiping over a highball

in a hot kitchen. I want to be told to stop
crinkling my nose at a hog maw
no one ever said I had to eat. I'm all about
brawling over a 25¢ hand of cards. I admit that

I'm not above jelly rolls and tea and backdoor pals,
the longing inherent in a departing train.
Please just hand me down some lovin'
tailor made for this bag of weary bones.

My heels are echoing on concrete,
a virtual percussion conjuring spring. The report
is just enough to tease me into
this conversation with myself.

SHOW, DON'T TELL

I'm a writer, I remind myself
over and over—I'm a writer, I'm a writer,
and I know the first rule: Show, don't tell.

Yet what do you do when they correct
the voice you've owned every day,
all your life, telling you *it's wrong*?

How do you hide exasperation
when no effort is made to mask
blatant biases? *It should be written this way.*

Why shield contempt from theory-
dense academics who note in red *I understand, but
why is the voice strident and shrill, angry?*

How do you show what they've seen
every day, all their lives, but still ignore?
Who made this rule? Not me, not mine.

Just once I want to show *and* tell,
so I can be sure they've seen and heard,
but just didn't give a damn.

IRONING IN JUNE

Gather the rudiments:
towel, damp cloth, spray
bottle of homemade sugar water
beneath the vault of a princess bed.

Wry and magnificent,
the insolent beast spits
a hiss of steam,
clearing its throat before the fall.

The smooth arc of the hilt,
contentious against the quilted
flesh of my palm,
strains to flatten a ruptured pleat.

My upper lip—skin supple,
saturated with humidity—
struggles to pardon
a single bead of sweat.

Such a tap dance. My mind wanders,
a gibbering scat. I coerce my attention
back to its task, having mastered
what my elders instilled.

Moisture and talcum assail
every crease a tomboy can hide.

Coup de grace: The beast lashes
its great, flagellating tail

around my arm. Every day, since
forever, I have known more burns than
forgiveness. I can't justify
these antiquated rituals. This heat tests
every fiber of my being.

BRAIDING ALEXIS

spraddled legs
    spidery blue skin
        a conflagration of tears

a living touchstone
by which to measure
generations of women

now voiceless
    now wordless
        speechless

I am perched behind you
attempting to part the dark
tunnels of glinting hair

you wince

uneasy   I want to say   it is the fault of the comb
the merciless   teeth   too close together
such a vast lie   will not forgather   without breath

you await
    straightbacked
        for the real pain to begin

with tenterhooks   I grapple flesh and bone
take hold   windblown strands
gone so far   awry

I hum   a discordant lullaby
thrummed   low in the throat
stories that have already begun   taking on veneer
children with fathers   raised   no better than bastards

a play cousin   a sister & an ex husband   questions of loyalty
a pistol in the choir stand   a heart & the philosophy   you broke
it, you bought it
keening wraiths scraped free of wombs   to escape   violent
flames
the ululant one   who relinquished loving   women for one man

even though I see the slippage
          my fingers keep moving
                    and though I am tempted

I will not begin again
          I say I am nearly finished
                    and ask if it's too tight

you continue weeping
          and shrug
                    unerring shoulders without blame

EQUINIMITY

Half-sleep, half-waked
my shutter eye clicks.
A room crowded with fringed lamps,
an antimacassared chair. A six-paneled door
grounded against thin vertical stripes.
Heavy oak dresser, a sepia-toned
lithograph of an actress. Delicate
white neck. Wicker chair
burdened with a mound of clothing.
African violets give birth
to a veritable jungle on the window ledge
as they drink polite sips of morning
light. The numbers turn slowly. Time almost
still. A rattan chest turned nightstand holds a
mason jar, filled with water, less
three small swallows. Damask and lace pillows.
Dust slanted blinds. Rows and rows of
books, most nursing cracked spines.
My breathing long as the mattress
is wide. The house settles and sighs.
The furnace's white noise has worried
the mauve candle away to hard, pink tears.
The swag of the valence forms an eye-
brow above a shaitan waterstain. We stare
at each other. Who will blink first?
I'm too scared to shut my eyes. Blink
closed. Darkness transmogrifies into stone
ladies with pubic hair manicured
more neatly than the lawn. Blink open.

My hips are cradled like a motherless child
where the sagging double bed dips.
This one time, the bent of memory
toward the absence of color.
You have to remember. I will
remember. I must remember.
I won't forget. My breath.
This room, this calm.

SALAH: DULLES AIRPORT

This is about my quiet fascination
with the man hidden behind the check-in desk.
He is bowing toward the wall.
I have to assume east is east.

The prayer rug he uses
is longer and has more colors
than my dress. He is oblivious
to how inappropriate I am.

He kneels, then stands,
then kneels, then stands.
His blue and white uniform
becomes flags upon the sea.

For less than a second, we lock
eyes. I am amazed by his beauty,
the meticulous calm with which he hobbles,
one leg shorter than the other—to duty free.

ODE TO SUE

for Langston

Theater crowd. Blaring lights.
A night surfeited with murmuring

voices. A cold wind licked shiny
bracelets around my ankles. I saw

a dark woman in a red dress. A vixen more
sure of herself than I had ever been.

Mouth, purse, nails, shoes—all red,
tantamount to blood on black soil.

I forgot where I was. What street
I was on. My breasts balled

into fists. My sex wept.
Somewhere, I knew

Susanna Jones smiled.

Ravished Landscapes

The thought of living
beyond my means,
holed up in a weather-beaten, white-
washed lean-to
amid rustling straw-blonde stalks
with the vast quietude of a century-
old oak to keep me company:

I push warm hominy
against the roof of my mouth,
thrusting my stealth tongue
upward through layers of whiteness
billowing like Illinois cumulus
—to see an inner clime of blue,
to taste some distant self.

I Can Show You

Put your finger on my
navel. Now wait,
close your eyes. Watch my stomach
muscles wilt, absorb my spine.

Cup your sandpaper hands
along the rise of my hips.
Flesh is a lie. Hold on. Feel. I can
take you to a country I can't pronounce.

Push everything from your mind, trust
I won't do you wrong. I wouldn't leave anybody
where I live. Most days, I'm low-bad and
this ain't nothing anyone wants to admit.

But for this minute, for this unending hour,
please, just be my witness. I can't tell you
where it is or how to get there, but if you can
withstand the detours, I can show you the way.

TRANSFIGURATION

The berth of the distant road calls
slow your roll, but bald tires speed,
racing alongside outcroppings of wisteria,
one length behind a waxing, alabaster moon.
Pull aside, woman, pull aside.

Stopped. Body rigid, belly flat.
First she opens the car door, then
soaked linen, button by pearl button,
laying bare dew-drenched skin.
—Is she the Black Madonna?

Heat slathers over her extremities
like wax, a steam descends, stripping
the irritating
vestiges of a dog day drive.
Pull aside, woman, pull aside

the moist cotton between
your thighs. Sponge clean
your sacrifice to the night.
Rivulets of love roux run dry.
"I am the Black Madonna."

She murmurs as mania leaps,
twirls between her shoulder blades.

Exhausted, she squats beneath a cypress.
With nature's ink, she draws shadows
in the dust—adoration for eternity.

HEAVY IN MY JESUS YEAR

I am of a nation of disbelievers. One of many
who only comes to geography by traveling.
Rhodesia became Zimbabwe, so they told me
the mothering instinct would come.

The stick turned a hesitant blue.

Cabbages, sweet onions, garlic, cayenne, and
beans. In some third-world nightmare,
women calling themselves friends admonished me
to straight-arm all comfort foods.

Brown women everywhere howled their sympathies.

You are born. The telling is easier when I forget
the gibbous bloom of your crown cut free of living rock:
broken water, fever, infection. Even flawed logic can be valid.
Pain has no reason but to give it voice.

A gasp. Months, no sleep. I dreamt of leaving your father.

Stretch marks mar my breasts like muck in a dry river-
bed—forsaken places made sane by a red August
heat. This summer, a woman called Yates did the
unspeakable, she crucified the last fairytale.

DISTANT NEIGHBOR

1.

There is an empty road between us.

2.

All she is a steady brow
peering out. Her bone-dry hand
shies away from the shattered glass
window of *what could have been.*

3.

Well-used but useless. Her
imagination strikes the first blow.
She is becoming a practiced gem
cutter, a vital tool skilled at finding
the clear blue flash in an emerald sky.

4.

Perhaps she will be able to coax her small son,
the refractory one with sand-colored eyes more liquid
than the asphalt sea he travels, for how does one
play at games more serious than honor?
Who knows, he might provide
the introductions culture requires.

5.

Our eyes ran from intimacy today and,
Sister, there is this thing I must say:
We have lost our lives,
yet here we are, amassing
a small fortune in indignities.

6.

I won't tell you that, in this country,
all you will ever be is black
robes hiding your low tolerance
for pleasure.
Try. Try *and* remember
the ripening dates and golden
figs that filled your days in Dubai.

7.

I divorce you.
I divorce you.
I . . . . We
are only women dreaming.
(Repeating this incantation
the third time will do no good.)
We should know by now; our
words hold no such magic.

8.

I strive toward boredom. I wear
my tattered dissatisfaction. I have spent
a snow-filled April with little more than
an agnostic's faith,

pinning all my hopes on mustard seeds:
Does anything in my gaze remind you of
some widowed aunt, some childhood friend?

9.
Dramatic, flowing behind
your garments float the air. You emerge,
reining in garbage cans.
A wolf alone in winter, you survey
the air, feigning not to notice
the bold one in the distance
who glows. The fire bidding welcome.

MUSTARD SEED
for R. V.

A sand road like a paper sky.
We will all become relics.
A kerosene tank, a rusted kiln,
a line of dust-white trucks and vans.
All threadbare. There is a lilting sign that touts
Cold Drinks. That is what
this landscape is. Fertile pines and wind.
Even now, in this beatific moment, a miraculous
depression rides me and death has lovely wrists.

A small oasis. Mud and mosquitoes
force me back to the pen. Such fruitless questions.
Pollen and germination. One speck
of truth buried beneath conjecture.
But I am left wondering if anyone ever
thought to, could have been bothered to,
hold her until she could calm her body
down. Did she have breathless
dreams of never being rescued? Night whispers its lie:
God never gives you more than you can handle.

Whatever. In the workshop ahead awaits the continual
moan of the fluorescent lights. Like an accusation,
the rhythmic logic of the blacksmith clangs. This
image. Singular. A reminder of how persistent is
the nature of shame. Shame on me, seeking an
answer where there is no pattern. I blink.
Insect bites ignored. I pad back to my rented room. I

resist the urge to scratch, to dial anyone who has ever
treated me well. Each busy signal,
each recorded voice, each silence becomes
another shovel of dirt.

SIMULACRA: GHAZAL AT 42

Each day hurts my skin, my mind. Upended, I try not to fall.
Today calls me back to untethered pain, the slow rain of fall.

I rejected my father's bluster. His childhood marred his mind.
He critiques all women, their physiques. I touch the noose and
fall.

The sky, I shatter with laughter—dry humor shakes loose my
skin.
With each *go fuck yourself*, I essay forth, Pirouette, pratfall.

Wending through forever, my yesteryears yip-yap after me.
I double-back, scowl, yell, "Turn back, now." In lust, again, I
fall.

Dear ewe, look inward, onward. Heart-grief rides beneath your
skin.
Words spiraling through blood and bone will never escape
nightfall.

UNDERTOW

The surface. A razor of rusted blue, hair-
thin, I thought I saw:
hope, faith size each other up,
avert eyes, part ways.

There is and is not
a method to this sadness.

The cell door caresses its track,
rushes shut. No key have I
found. Reason, my love, cannot fathom
when she might find time enough

to tend my needs. Again, my gentle anguish
cannot cobble together
anything resembling rage.

Decency, the ninny, asks that I float
letters home, just one or three,
maybe a fistful or so, to let
mama, daddy, sister, brother,

husband, sons know
I'm *alright.* I'm not. I cannot

manage to take hold of a thought
much less string together such long nights
and days filled with fear. I won't tell anyone

how I've lost count of days served
and can't keep track of when or where
amid the labyrinth
next the parole board meets.
A dysphoric appeal? Certainly not

malicious, not benign. Almost, not quite
contrite, the moon deigns to pat my shoulder,
as she shakes her head. My mind is locked,
caged in a room on a foundered rig,
indebted to voracious lungs, cracked wineskins,
resentful of the sky, filling with the undertow.

Her Lover Eyes the Exit

A madman's creation, she is what she is,
    at once, both wolf and bitch.
        She fills the red corners of my eyes

even when she is not there. I feel her
    nails grip the flesh over my clavicles
        like rusted hooks. My thighs are solemn

between hers—a fierce stillness,
    a tender vise. Her tongue
        grates like sandpaper but can weave itself

into a swirling tapestry of silk. Nothing I can do
    will ever be enough. No amount of silence
        holds back her waves of pain.

But when she says *I am yours,*
    butterflies alight on my eyelids.
        And the unbearable longing is over.

The apologies that will never come
    take wing for one bitter, blessèd moment,
        then are gone.

AUBADE

There was no sex involved. I went
barefoot,
down to the kitchen. And there,
a reflection faced me, gaunt
in the light of the sliding glass door,
perched
in the plastic-covered white chair.
She, whittling dawn
as one contemplates the tart
pit of a nectarine. Her
gown fell open.
Her brow like a crate
—low, short, square.
Her breasts were still
reasonably small. She was beating back
that understandable need to flee.
She sat poised, trained, coiled
like a sprinter's inner watch, wound
tighter than tight,
anticipating the gun. What did she say but . . .
"This isn't what I signed on for.
This ain't what you promised."
I could've lied to her,
told that comely woman
that I was the same person
I used to be, that just around the corner
was gonna be some lewd
blue lights and scandal. No,

that life was over.
No need to be
pretending for this other, younger
version of who I once was.
I confessed, "This it . . . this
is all there is.
Babies, a man, a mortgage, and groceries.
Now
do what you gotta.
Go,
if you must."

SIGHTLINES

While driving, I continually force
myself to see what lies afore and behind.

Landmarks, edges.
Time, space, distance. I am constant

in my distractions. Blessed with eyes
that cannot see

the sense of always running
to serve an unrelenting wreck of small favors

that busies us all—until death. This thought,
fleeting as clarity: my soul I must guard.

An obscene wind whips my car
toward the center line. My grip tightens

on this wintry afternoon; it's almost night.
I venture the horizon, bleak joy of midlife. I follow

the crosshatch of wires racing the landscape.
My mind narrows down, chasing a gaudy riot of flowers,

a pushpin holding down a memory. A life
made concrete by this paltry marker

hidden on the graveled shoulder of a north Texas road.
So, this is eternity. Fake flowers—and no name.

HEATHEN

"I can't save you." Nature
tamps the imprint of a rotting leaf
upon concrete. Her man thinks and sighs
sighs and thinks. "What can you do
with a woman who won't
do what you say?" *You love her.*

The snow is falling. He's cold.
Like her. This weather is teeters between
brutal and fierce. *I can't make you
understand what I need.* He
mumbles. "I couldn't save her
even if I wanted." This, at least,

feels like an attempt. There are hours
when the world almost makes sense
to him. His legs scissored between
hers. Her hips bearing down. Grinding
like a pestle against mortar. Once,
long ago, he tattooed his name inside her.

A piece of ice is breaking
free of the gable. Right now,
he's asleep. She cares but doesn't
care. She will wake him. *Come on, now.
Please. It's too cold to take a shower.*
"This once, tell me I'm what you want."

HERE

Here, the task of surviving winter:
I rededicate myself to pornographic seed
catalogs, look out the patio window upon
frost-destroyed joe-pye and dying flames of canna
crusted over with each morning's frost.

Here, I begin to tell myself lies: I am not cold,
that the sun will return, that the bare brown limb isn't
actually God's finger, indicting me to endure
suburban dictates of normative hypocrisies.
I close my mind and plot rebellion:

I wonder if I can make the Himalayan blue poppy bloom
here in Texas. I behold my mind's upheavals
amid the ice and distant neighbors' lights.
I dream each night of the March planting date, try not to
count the seventy-six days until common sense returns.

January will find me forty-two and for once
not wholly blue but content with the muted sun.
Here, the wind whispers its lies and
any misery becomes a prostitute for my regrets.
I bite the dead skin from my lips.

Gardening in winter: a fluke day of 68 degrees and sun.
I hack and hack, attacking all that has died. This act
requires faith: that seeds have ripened and fallen,

that the roots have taken hold, that the mulch
will protect. I hear the freezing of the land, which

is the hardening of my heart. Inside,
exhausted, I swirl the fleece blanket overhead
and around my shoulders. Always ready for a fight,
I speak. I regard the wind, the night,
then listen for the thaw, for spring. Here.

About the Author

R. Flowers Rivera is a native of Mississippi. She completed a Ph.D. in English, specializing in African American literature and creative writing, at Binghamton University and an M.A. in English at Hollins University. She also earned an M.S. in human resource development from Georgia State University and a B.S. from The University of Georgia.

Xavier Review Press published her debut poetry collection, *Troubling Accents* (2013), which received a nomination in poetry for *Troubling Accents* from the Mississippi Institute of Arts and Letters and was selected by the Texas Association of Authors as its 2014 Poetry Book of the Year. Rivera's second collection, *Heathen*, was selected by poet and literary activist E. Ethelbert Miller as this year's winner of the Naomi Long Madgett Poetry Award. Rivera's work limns and re-imagines the intersections of race, gender, class, orientation, and regional identity.

Rivera was awarded the 2009 Leo Love Merit Scholarship in Poetry in association with the Taos Summer Writers Conference. Her short story, "The Iron Bars," won the 1999 Peregrine Prize, and she was a finalist for the May Swenson Award, the Journal Intro Award, the Gary Snyder Memorial Award, the Paumanok Award, the Crab Orchard Series, and the Gival Poetry Prize, as well as garnering nominations for Pushcarts. Rivera has been anthologized in *Mischief, Caprice & Other Poetic Strategies* and included in a book on poetics entitled *The Rhythm Method, Razzmatazz and Poetry*. She has been published in journals such as *African American Review, Columbia, Evergreen Chronicles, Beloit Poetry Journal, Feminist Studies, Obsidian, The Southern Review*, and *UCity Review*. She currently lives in McKinney, Texas.

CRITICAL PRAISE

"In language that sweeps from high lyric to downhome vernacular, R. Flowers Rivera undertakes the always more necessary work of re-weaving the ancient tales back into our daily lives. In doing so, she quietly makes a radical claim: that our lives cease to be as real as they can be when we neglect to recognize in them, not the every day chores of work and life, but the reality that comes when we can no longer ignore what is easiest to deny, that some aspect of myth's timelessness weaves itself throughout the mundane. It is a vision—and so are these poems—whose reminder to us is one we must be grateful for: what is past has not passed, and the old gods go on living their lives within our own."

> —Dan Beachy-Quick, author of *North True Bright.Spell,*
> *Mulberry, This Nest,* and *Swift Passerine*

" 'A sudden blow' is how Yeats famously described Zeus's rape of Leda. R. Flowers Rivera revisits this scene (and many others) but eschews Yeats's cool third-person reportage. Instead, Rivera's Leda talks to her younger self, telling her that soon, she 'will begin to waste / slow hours watching the horizon.' What follows seems a textbook description of trauma, and while Yeats never shied away from such psychological probings into myth, Rivera appears to take that act as her chief concern. No, retelling mythical and biblical stories is nothing new. When they are this good, however, who cares?"

> —Chad Davidson, author of *From the Fire Hills,*
> *The Last Predicta,* and *Consolation Miracle*

"R. Flowers Rivera's book, *Heathen,* is amazing work. It includes many persona poems based on mythology, but the voices are so down-home, so real, so irreverent and alive, that they lack all pretension, the kind of pretension that is too often present in persona poems. Other poems in this stunningly

113

beautiful collection allude to the Bible and to literary figures, yet all the poems have a clarity of vision, a sureness of voice that makes them unforgettable."

"In *Heathen*, R. Flowers Rivera remixes the classical and the Biblical, the usual and the typical until what we thought we knew of ourselves and others is new again. The mythic becomes particular; the particular becomes mythic in these fascinating poems of personalities and personas. Rivera's work is rich in empathy and invention. *Heathen* is a book of psalms for the present day."

"Rivera's poems contain multitudes. Even when she speaks through the masks of Greek mythic figures, a voice that is Southern and female and humanly desiring erupts through the cracks. What all of her poetic selves have in common is a preference for reckless action over tedium, and that makes for excitement on the page. Hugely gifted, R. Flowers Rivera is a talent to watch."